Peppa Pig™

Happy Holiday

Activity Book

This book
belongs to:

....

Time to Pack

Peppa and George are packing for their holiday! Trace over the letters to see which is their favourite toy.

dinosaur

teddy

3

Let's Fly!

Help Peppa and her family fly through the sky.
How many fluffy white clouds can you count?

Start

4

Finish

On the Road

Daddy Pig is driving to the holiday house, but he's going the wrong way! Spot five differences between the two pictures and draw a circle around each one.

A

B

Answers: 1. The family suitcase is missing in picture B. 2. The sun has moved across the sky in picture B. 3. There are four clouds in picture B. 4. In picture B, the car at the bottom right is purple. 5. In picture A, the truck is empty.

Wonderful Writing

Finish off the words below with some beautiful 'b's!

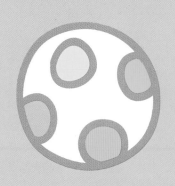

ball   balloon   boots

book   bananas   bag

Answers: There are three bunches of grapes and four oranges.

Splash!

Oh no, Daddy Pig has fallen into the swimming pool in his pyjamas! Poor Daddy Pig!

How many bunches of grapes can you count?

How many oranges can you count?

Shopping Fun

Peppa is shopping for presents. Look at the six little pictures in the panel and find them in the big picture. When you find each object, colour the shiny gold coin next to it.

Picture Postcards

Peppa and George love drawing pictures and sending them to their family and friends. Use these simple templates so you can do the same.

What to do:
1. Draw pictures in the white spaces labelled 'Side A', then cut them out and stick them on to thin card. Ask a grown-up to help you.

Side A

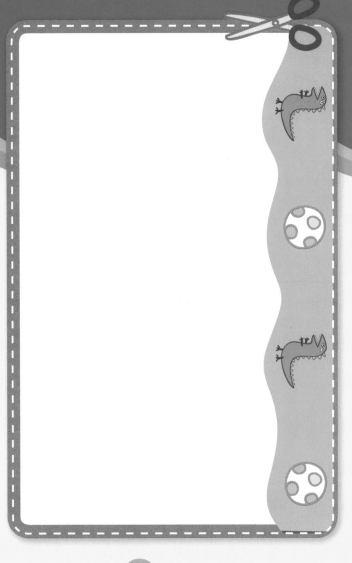

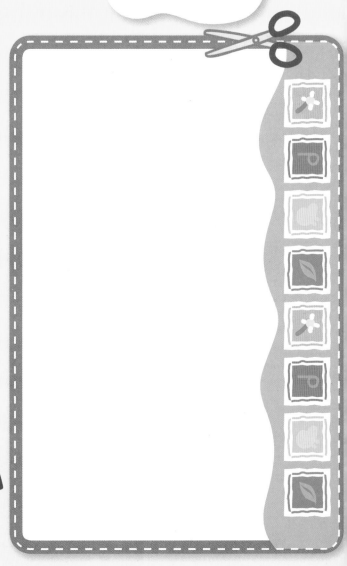

2. Ask a grown-up to help you write the name and address of who you would like to send your pictures to on the lines of 'Side B'. Cut these out and stick them on the back of your 'Side A' pictures.

Side B

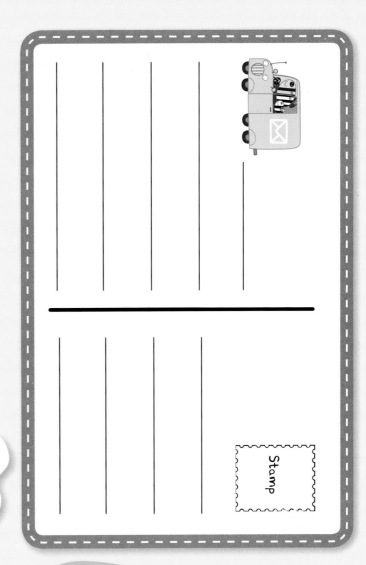

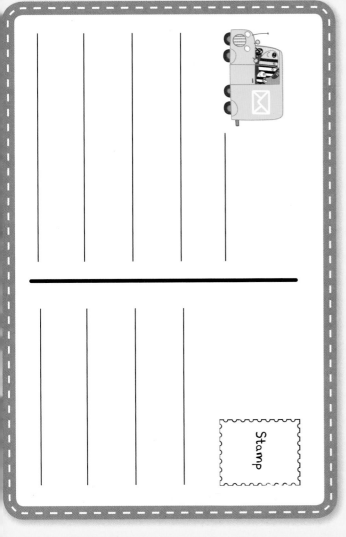

Stamp

3. Put a stamp in the small box, then post your picture! If you don't have a stamp you can hand-deliver it instead.

Peppa's Postcard

Mummy Pig is helping Peppa write a postcard to Goldie the goldfish. Can you draw a picture on the postcard and colour it in?

Pen Pals

Peppa has a pen pal called Delphine Donkey.
She lives in France! Peppa has drawn a lovely picture
for Delphine. She gives it to Mr Zebra to deliver.

Mr Zebra hasn't been to France before.
Can you decide which road he should take?

A

B

C

ANSWER: C

Home Again!

Peppa is sad that the holiday is over, but jumping in puddles will cheer her up! How many muddy splats can you count in the picture? Snort! Snort!

Answer: There are ten muddy splats.